Best Wishes!!

David Holland

Phil McKerrey

THE PRESIDENTS IN QUIRKY ILLUSTRATED VERSE

Verses by

DAVID HOLLAND

Illustrations by

PHIL MCKENNEY

Fulton Books
Meadville, PA

Published by Fulton Books 2022

ISBN 978-1-63985-473-8 (hardcover)
ISBN 978-1-63985-472-1 (digital)

Printed in the United States of America

To Josie, AJ, Esther, and JJ, as selected in random order.

And in memory of Lucy and Phillip McKenney.

INTRODUCTION

Why poke a little fun at America's presidents? Well, why not? Being able to laugh at your leaders is a sign of a free country. And laughter just might help keep those leaders' feet on the ground.

America is currently on its forty-sixth president. A few of them have been presidents of accomplishment and distinction, perhaps most notably George Washington, Abraham Lincoln, and Franklin Roosevelt. Others were generally successful but were not seriously challenged by the events of their terms. Still others were adequate or, no names please, subpar. Several, again no names, were ill-equipped intellectually, managerially, morally, or all three, to be leaders of a vibrant, diverse, often chaotic nation.

The Presidents in Quirky Illustrated Verse summarizes the, to date, forty-six US presidents. The summaries are through quirky poetry and even quirkier art. Will the reader emerge with an in-depth knowledge of the forty-six presidents? No, that is a task for Wikipedia. But the reader might acquire a tidbit or so that could be dropped into a conversation and maybe foster an impression of advanced erudition. Hey, that last sentence has a quirky rhyme!

THE PRESIDENTS CHRONOLOGICALLY

1) George Washington, 1789–1797
2) John Adams, 1797–1801
3) Thomas Jefferson, 1801–1809
4) James Madison, 1809–1817
5) James Monroe, 1817–1825
6) John Quincy Adams, 1825–1829
7) Andrew Jackson, 1829–1837
8) Martin Van Buren, 1837–1841
9) William Henry Harrison, 1841–1841
10) John Tyler, 1841–1845
11) James K. Polk, 1845–1849
12) Zachary Taylor, 1849–1850
13) Millard Fillmore, 1850–1853
14) Franklin Pierce, 1853–1857
15) James Buchanan, 1857–1861
16) Abraham Lincoln, 1861–1865
17) Andrew Johnson, 1865–1869
18) Ulysses S. Grant, 1869–1877
19) Rutherford B. Hayes, 1877–1881
20) James A. Garfield, 1881–1881
21) Chester A. Arthur, 1881–1885
22) Grover Cleveland, 1885–1889
23) Benjamin Harrison, 1889–1893
24) Grover Cleveland, 1893–1897
25) William McKinley, 1897–1901
26) Theodore Roosevelt, 1901–1909
27) William Howard Taft, 1909–1913
28) Woodrow Wilson, 1913–1921
29) Warren G. Harding, 1921–1923
30) Calvin Coolidge, 1923–1929
31) Herbert Hoover, 1929–1933
32) Franklin D. Roosevelt, 1933–1945
33) Harry S. Truman, 1945–1953
34) Dwight David Eisenhower, 1953–1961
35) John F. Kennedy, 1961–1963
36) Lyndon B. Johnson, 1963–1969
37) Richard Nixon, 1969–1974

38) Gerald Ford, 1974–1977
39) Jimmy Carter, 1977–1981
40) Ronald Reagan, 1981–1989
41) George H.W. Bush, 1989–1993
42) Bill Clinton, 1993–2001
43) George W. Bush, 2001–2009
44) Barack Obama, 2009–2017
45) Donald J. Trump, 2017–2021
46) Joe Biden, 2021-Present

THE PRESIDENTS ALPHABETICALLY

Adams, John, #2, 1797–1801
Adams, John Quincy, #6, 1825–1829
Arthur, Chester A., #21, 1881–1885
Biden, Joe, #46, 2021-Present
Buchanan, James, #15, 1857–1861
Bush, George H. W., #41, 1989–1993
Bush, George W., #43, 2001–2009
Carter, Jimmy, #39, 1977–1981
Cleveland, Grover, #22, 1885–1889
Cleveland, Grover, #24, 1893–1897
Clinton, Bill, #42, 1993–2001
Coolidge, Calvin, #30, 1923–1929
Eisenhower, Dwight David, #34, 1953–1961
Fillmore, Millard, #13, 1850–1853
Ford, Gerald, #38, 1974–1977
Garfield, James A., #20, 1881–1881
Grant, Ulysses S., #18, 1869–1877
Harding, Warren G., #29, 1921–1923
Harrison, Benjamin, #23, 1889–1893
Harrison, William Henry, #9, 1841–1841
Hayes, Rutherford B., #19, 1877–1881
Hoover, Herbert, # 31, 1929–1933
Jackson, Andrew, #7, 1829–1837
Jefferson, Thomas, #3, 1801–1809
Johnson, Andrew, #17, 1865–1869
Johnson, Lyndon B., #36, 1963–1969
Kennedy, John F., #35, 1961–1963
Lincoln, Abraham, #16, 1861–1865
Madison, James, #4, 1809–1817
McKinley, William, #25, 1897–1901
Monroe, James, #5, 1817–1825
Nixon, Richard, #37, 1969–1974
Obama, Barack, #44, 2009–2017
Pierce, Franklin, #14, 1853–1857
Polk, James K., #11, 1845–1849
Reagan, Ronald, #40, 1981–1989
Roosevelt, Franklin D., #32, 1933–1945

Roosevelt, Theodore, #26, 1901–1909
Taft, William Howard, #27, 1909–1913
Taylor, Zachary, #12, 1849–1850
Truman, Harry S., #33, 1945–1953
Trump, Donald J., #45, 2017–2021
Tyler, John, #10, 1841–1845
Van Buren, Martin, #8, 1837–1841
Washington, George, #1, 1789–1797
Wilson, Woodrow, #28, 1913–1921

GEORGE WASHINGTON

1ST PRESIDENT
1789–1797
Party: Unaffiliated
b. 1732, d. 1799

George Washington is often called
The Father of his Country
He was a Virginia planter
Businessman and slave owner
Statesman and soldier

He commanded the Continental Army
During the American Revolution
And presided in 1787 over the
Constitutional Convention

Slavery was pervasive in
And fundamental to
The southern American colonies
And remained so after
The colonies from Great Britain withdrew

This deeply rooted flaw
In the American story
Led eventually to civil war
And is a blemish on American glory

Washington was not perfect
But he was an even-tempered man
Calm and reasonable
In a turbulent land

Not all his successors
Met the standards he set
For being a successful
President

PROUD PAPA

JOHN ADAMS

2ND PRESIDENT
1797–1801
Party: Federalist
b. 1735, d. 1826

John Adams of Massachusetts
Was an attorney and writer
A delegate to the Continental Congress
And a Declaration of Independence drafter and signer

After the Declaration was signed
He had diplomatic roles in Europe
He was a negotiator
Of the 1783 treaty ending the war
And in 1785 became
America's Great Britain Ambassador

Despite a prickly personality
He became America's first vice president
Serving for Washington's two terms
And in 1797 became the second president

He lost the 1800 election
To his once-friend, Tom Jefferson
But the relationship was mended eventually
And in their later years, they corresponded extensively

Both Adams and Jefferson
Passed away on July 4, 1826
Fifty years to the day
After the Declaration of Independence

THOMAS JEFFERSON

3RD PRESIDENT
1801–1809
Party: Democratic-Republican
b. 1743, d. 1826

Thomas Jefferson of Virginia
Was a planter, writer, diplomat
Founding Father, slave owner
Statesman, philosopher, architect

A multitalented individual
He was the principal author
Of the Declaration of Independence
And a staunch religious freedom supporter

In his two terms
The Louisiana Purchase was made
Western expeditions including Lewis and Clark were conducted
And relations with Great Britain decayed

From the view of the Twenty-First Century
Jefferson's position on slavery
Lacked much clarity
He owned slaves but signed legislation
Outlawing the slave trade internationally

After leaving the presidency
Jefferson avoided much political strife
He established the University of Virginia
(Which after almost two centuries
Would become a hoops power)
And maintained an active life

JAMES MADISON

4TH PRESIDENT
1809–1817
Party: Democratic-Republican
b. 1751, d. 1836

James Madison was another
Multitalented Founding Father
Statesman, diplomat, slave owner
From the state of Virginia

He played a major role
In the 1787 Philadelphia Convention
And authored with Alexandria Hamilton and John Jay
The Federalist Papers describing the Constitution

He also was a leader
In the adoption of the first Ten Amendments
Called the Bill of Rights and focused
On the protection of individual independence

During Jefferson's presidency
Madison was Secretary of State
Three years after becoming president
War with Great Britain fell onto his plate

Although America failed to take Canada
And the Brits burned Washington
The War of 1812 ended on a high note
With the Battle of New Orleans
Won by Andrew Jackson

Madison's wife, Dolly
Helped define the role of First Lady
The last years of his presidency
Were the "Era of Good Feelings"
Although there was considerable debate about
The legality and extent of federal spending

JAMES MONROE

5TH PRESIDENT
1817–1825
Party: Democratic-Republican
b. 1758, d. 1831

James Monroe was the fourth Virginian
To become president
He wasn't quite a Founding Father
But he was a wounded
Revolutionary War soldier

He was a Secretary of State under Madison
And during Jefferson's presidency
Helped negotiate
The Louisiana Purchase transaction

As with his three Virginia predecessors
He was a slave owner
He supported the return
Of freed slaves to Africa
And the capital of Liberia
Is named for him, Monrovia

As president, he issued the Monroe Doctrine
Saying European nations
Should no longer consider
The Western Hemisphere open to colonization
He also acquired
Florida from Spain
And encouraged Western expansion

He was the last president to wear
In eighteenth century format
A powdered wig, tricornered hat, and knee breeches
Earning him the nickname,
"The Last Cocked Hat"

JOHN QUINCY ADAMS

6TH PRESIDENT
Party: Democratic-Republican; National Republican
1825–1829
b. 1767, d. 1848

John Quincy Adams of Massachusetts
Finally brought
The Virginia Dynasty
To a halt

The son of John Adams
The second president
John Quincy had a term
In the US Senate
Was Secretary of State under James Monroe
Had diplomatic experience
So was ready to go

As president, he had
An extensive domestic agenda
Which had only modest success
Against the congressional meat grinder

He was committed to
Western expansion
Wore long pants
And short hair was his fashion

He served nine terms in Congress
After the presidency
During his congressional career
He was increasingly critical of slavery

ANDREW JACKSON

7TH PRESIDENT
Party: Democratic
1829–1837
b. 1767, d. 1845

After four decades of
Virginia and Massachusetts intellectuals
The presidency in 1829
Expanded its membership to others
Even scoundrels and rascals

Andrew Jackson of Tennessee
Was the first of the new breed
A lawyer, slave owner, and militia leader
He rode a different stead

He led troops
In various conflicts with Native Americans
And in the War of 1812
He beat the British at New Orleans

As President, he authorized the expulsion
Of Native Americans from much of the South
He forced the Second Bank of the United States
Into termination
Which opened the economy to
The 1837 panic and devastation
He paid off the national debt
(The last time that has happened)
And he left in his wake
Considerable division

His tenure has been described
As the common man versus the corrupt aristocracy
A theme that has waxed and waned
Through much of the nation's subsequent history

MARTIN VAN BUREN

8TH PRESIDENT
Party: Democratic
1837–1841
b. 1782, d. 1862

Martin Van Buren was from New York
Of Dutch heritage, he was a lawyer
Was active in New York politics
Including seven years as a US Senator

He was a believer
In a political party system
With parties separated by policy differences
Rather than personal ambition

The election of 1836
Marked the solidification
Of the two-party system
With the Democratic party on one side
And the Whigs in opposition

Van Buren was a Democratic President
But not a particularly successful one
His tenure was hampered by
An extended depression

Although at one time
He had owned a slave
He opposed the annexation of Texas
Fearing the extension of slavery
Would be for the nation very reckless

He struggled with the banking system
And continued the removal of Native Americans
From the Southern States
Although the Seminoles in Florida
Fought him to a stalemate

WILLIAM HENRY HARRISON

9TH PRESIDENT
Party: Whig
1841–1841
b. 1773, d. 1841

William Henry Harrison
Was a Virginian
Who spent much of his life
In the Northwest Territory
And ended up an Ohioan

He had a variety of government and military positions
Signed a number of treaties with Native Americans
Won a victory over the Shawnee
At the battle of Tippecanoe
And in the War of 1812
Won victories over the British too

In the election of 1840
He ran as a Whig
With John Tyler as his number two
Their campaign slogan was
"Tippecanoe and Tyler, Too"

His two-hour inaugural address
Was the longest on record
The day was cold, wet, and a nasty mess
He became ill and set another record
The shortest tenure, one month
Wearing the presidential vest

JOHN TYLER

10TH PRESIDENT
Party: Whig, Unaffiliated
1841–1845
b. 1790, d. 1862

When William Henry Harrison
Died after a month in office
VP John Tyler became President
Much to many Whig's disgust

Tyler was a Virginian and slave owner
Had served as a state legislator
Had been the Governor, a US Representative
And a US Senator

Much of Harrison's cabinet resigned
Soon into Tyler's term
Whigs dubbed him "His Accidency"
And expelled him from the party

Tyler signed some bills
Of the Whig-controlled Congress
But he vetoed tariff and national bank measures
Because he was a strict constructionist

He had more success
In the foreign affairs area
Texas annexation authorized
A treaty with China
Applying the Monroe Doctrine to Hawaii
Border dispute settled between Maine and Canada

JAMES K. POLK

11TH PRESIDENT
Party: Democratic
1845–1849
b. 1795, d. 1849

James K. Polk
Was born in North Carolina
But raised in Tennessee
He was a slave owner
And an advocate of Jeffersonian Democracy

Polk was in the House of Representatives
From 1825 to 1839
He was Speaker of the House
For the last years of that time

He was Governor of Tennessee
For a short interval
Then became the first "dark horse" president
Describing an event some did ridicule

He made a major contribution
To American lore
Expanding the nation's borders
To the Pacific shore

In the Mexican-American War
He solidified the Texas annexation
And he settled with Great Britain
The Oregon Territory border frustration

ZACHARY TAYLOR

12TH PRESIDENT
Party: Whig
1849–1850
b. 1784, d. 1850

Zachary Taylor was born in Virginia
Raised in Kentucky
And in later life had ties to
Louisiana and Mississippi

He was a professional soldier
Fought in multiple conflicts
1812, Mexican-American, Second Seminole
Was nicknamed "Old Rough and Ready"
And was a hero to many

Taylor was a slave owner
But did not push slavery expansion
Thought it was impractical in the West
He explicitly opposed suggestions
Of Southern secession

He was in office
Just a little more than a year
During 1850 July 4th celebrations
He consumed too much raw fruit and iced milk
And succumbed to maybe diarrhea

His major presidential accomplishment
Was a treaty with Great Britain
Concerning Central America
But having the long-term effect
Of solidifying the Anglo-American connection

MILLARD FILLMORE

13TH PRESIDENT
Party: Whig
1850–1853
b. 1800, d. 1874

Millard Fillmore was raised
In rural New York
He was a lawyer and politician
And served eight years
In the US House of Representatives

He became President
Upon Zachery Taylor's death
Those years were dominated
By the slavery issue mess

Fillmore considered slavery an evil
But viewed it as beyond the purview
Of the federal government's ability
To judge and review

The Compromise of 1850
Was the major product of his administration
Ultimately a failed attempt
To prevent the coming War of Secession

Millard did not get
The Whig nomination in 1852
He did get the Know-Nothing nomination
In 1856
But lost the election

FRANKLIN PIERCE

14TH PRESIDENT
Party: Democratic
1853–1857
b. 1804, d. 1869

Franklin Pierce was a lawyer and politician
He was from New Hampshire
From 1833 to 1842 he was in the US Congress
First as a Representative and then a Senator

As a Brigadier General
In the Mexican-American belligerency
He was an adequate leader
But injuries limited his activity

Most notably he slammed his groin
Into the horn on his saddle
Then his horse fell on him
Leaving him with quite a waddle

He believed that the abolitionist movement
Was a threat to the unity of the nation
As President, he supported the Kansas-Nebraska Act
Which nullified the Missouri Compromise
And set the stage for the coming destruction

He perfected the comb over
And was a heavy drinker
His death in 1869 was due to
Cirrhosis of the liver

JAMES BUCHANAN

15TH PRESIDENT
Party: Democratic
1857–1861
b. 1791, d. 1868

James Buchanan was the only President
(Until Joe Biden) from Pennsylvania
Also the only President to be
A lifelong bachelor
And the only President with military experience
(in the War of 1812)
Not as an officer

He was a lawyer and politician
Served in both Houses of Congress
And as a foreign diplomat
And in the Secretary of State position

The slavery and secession issues
Dominated his term
He thought slavery a matter for the states
And his views about secession were not firm

He supported the Supreme Court's
Dred Scott Decision
That Black individuals were not entitled
To the rights and privileges of the Constitution

He believed secession was not
In a state's authority
But preventing secession was not
A proper federal activity

By the time his term ended
The nation was ready
To shed copious blood
And endure the deaths of many

ABRAHAM LINCOLN

16TH PRESIDENT
Party: Republican; National Union
1861–1865
b. 1809, d. 1865

Presidents of the preceding few decades
Had mostly been average
But as the nation fell into the abyss
Of slavery, secession, sectional aggression
Presidential luck reversed
His name was Abraham Lincoln

"Honest Abe" was from Kentucky
Grew up in Indiana and settled in Illinois
He was a lawyer, politician, and an avid reader
Was tall and had great poise

The election of Lincoln in 1860
As the first Republican President
Triggered the attempted secession of Southern States
Unhappy with the antislavery environment

Lincoln opposed secession
Wanting to hold the nation together
Thus, the Civil War began
After more than six hundred thousand deaths
The Union won, and the nation remained one

With the Emancipation Proclamation
And the Thirteenth Amendment
Lincoln brought an end
To the slavery entanglement

As the war was ending
And his second term beginning
Lincoln was assassinated
Leaving the nation reeling

ANDREW JOHNSON

17TH PRESIDENT
Party: National Union; Democratic
1865–1869
b. 1808, d. 1875

Andrew Johnson was born in North Carolina
Moved to Tennessee where he worked as a tailor
Became a politician, served in the US House,
As state Governor and as a US Senator

He was the only senator
Of a seceding state
Who remained with the Union
Rather than embrace a treasonous fate

He owned a few slaves
But during the war, he set them free
Lincoln appointed him
Military Governor of Tennessee

In the election of 1864
He received the VP selection
And became President
Upon Lincoln's assassination

He was stubborn and uncompromising
And rebelled against Congress' directives
That challenged his lenient
Reconstruction policies
He was impeached but not convicted
The only President impeached
In the nation's first two centuries

RUTHERFORD B. HAYES

19TH PRESIDENT
Party: Republican
1877–1881
b. 1822, d. 1893

Rutherford B. Hayes was from Ohio
Was a lawyer and staunch abolitionist
His law practice included defending slaves
Who fled from their owners saying
Enough of this mess

Hayes fought in the Civil War
In the Western Virginia vicinity
Was wounded five times
Attained the rank of Brevet Major General
And the admiration of the citizenry

After serving in the US House
And as Governor of Ohio
He was elected President
In the most contentious election
In the history of the nation

Disturbed by drunken behavior
And influenced by his temperate spouse
Derogatorily known as "Lemonade Lucy"
He banned liquor from the White House

Issues during his presidency included
Increasing the coinage in circulation
The Great Railroad Strike of 1877
And civil service reform legislation

HAYES
CABINET

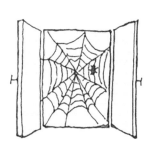

HAYES
LIQUOR CABINET

JAMES A. GARFIELD

20TH PRESIDENT
Party: Republican
1881–1881
b. 1831, d. 1881

James A. Garfield has been called
The last log cabin president
He was a lawyer and politician
Born in Ohio, he remained a resident

In the early years of the Civil War
He fought at Middle Creek, Shiloh
And Chickamauga
He attained the rank of Major General
And the interest of politicians in Ohio

He was elected in 1862
To the House of Representatives
Initially a Radical Republican
He gradually moderated his views
On civil rights enforcement and Reconstruction

In 1880, he became
The only sitting House member to be elected
President of the country
Among his concerns were
Civil service reform, civil rights for Black Americans
And presidential authority

After just a few months in office
He was shot by a disgruntle job seeker
Becoming the second president assassinated
When he died several months later

CHESTER A. ARTHUR

21ST PRESIDENT
Party: Republican
1881–1885
b. 1829, d. 1886

Upon the death of James A. Garfield
Chester A. Arthur succeeded to the presidency
He was born in Vermont
Spent his youth in upstate New York
And practiced law in New York City

In the Civil War he served
In quartermaster roles with the New York militia
And in 1871 was appointed
Collector of the Port of New York
A lucrative position
In an organization of corrupt inertia

Though honorable personally and in his career
He was nevertheless a firm believer
In the spoils system regime
He properly administered the New York Custom House
Except for overstaffing it with appointees
From his party's patronage machine

As President, he tried to rise above
The political and government corruption of the times
He succeeded to a degree
But the post-Civil War decades
Of the nineteenth century
Would have filled a certain much later President
With considerable envy

As President, he became a champion
Of civil service reform, approved an immigration law
Modernized the Navy, tried to lower tariffs
And said no polygamy for Utah

GROVER CLEVELAND

22ND PRESIDENT
Party: Democratic
1885–1889
b. 1837, d. 1908

Grover Cleveland was born in Vermont
Raised in New York
Avoided Civil War conscription
Through a hired substitution

He was a lawyer in Buffalo
Then the Mayor, then Governor of the state
He became the first Democratic President
Since the Civil War did terminate

A child out of wedlock
Was an issue in the 1884 election
Cleveland's opposition had a chant
"Ma, Ma, Where's my Pa?"
After the election, his supporters responded
"Gone to the White House, Ha! Ha! Ha!"

Cleveland arrived in Washington a bachelor
But he ended that situation
By marrying the daughter of a friend
She was twenty-one, Grover, the old fox, was forty-nine
But apparently in good condition

To paraphrase one description
Cleveland was praised for his honesty
Integrity and classical liberalism
He fought political corruption, patronage, and bossism
He was reluctant to spend
And prolifically wielded the veto pen

BENJAMIN HARRISON

23RD PRESIDENT
Party: Republican
1889–1893
b. 1833, d. 1901

Benjamin Harrison was a lawyer and politician
Born in Ohio, he became an Indiana resident
He was the grandson of William Henry Harrison
The ninth president

During the Civil War
Harrison was in the military
He participated in Sherman's Atlanta campaign
Commanding the 70th Indiana Infantry

He served in the Senate in the 1880s
As President, he pushed a vigorous foreign policy
Established the forerunner of the Pan American Union
And is generally viewed as acting with integrity

Legislation during his presidency included
The Sherman Antitrust Act regulating trusts
And the McKinley Tariff imposing
Historically high protective tariffs

During Harrison's term
Electricity was installed in the White House
But he and his wife were afraid of the switches
And often slept with the lights on
Rather than tempt the electric witches

GROVER CLEVELAND

24TH PRESIDENT
Party: Democratic
1893–1897
b. 1837, d. 1908

Yes, this is the same Grover
As number twenty-two
The only president to leave town
Then return for another round

He won the popular vote
In the election of '88
But that mean 'ol Electoral College
Kept him from the finish gate

By 1892, however
The high tariffs of the Republicans
Had made imported goods very costly
Cleveland won by wide margins
A popular and electoral victory

But shortly after his second term began
The stock market and economy
Were inconveniently hammered by
The Panic of 1893

Cleveland spent his second term
Dealing mostly with economic matters
Silver, tariffs, the Pullman Strike
Left his political support in tatters

WILLIAM MCKINLEY

25TH PRESIDENT
Party: Republican
1897–1901
b. 1843, d. 1901

William McKinley was born and raised in Ohio
A lawyer and politician
He was the last president to be
A Civil War veteran

He entered the military as a private
Achieving Brevet Major ultimately
He had a horse shot from under him
And fought at Antietam and in the Shenandoah Valley

McKinley served fourteen years in the House
And two terms as Ohio Governor
In the House, he was the leading Republican tariff expert
And as President produced the highest US tariff ever

Foreign affairs dominated his presidency
In the Spanish-American War
He led the nation to victory
Achieving independence for Cuba and annexing
The Philippines, Guam, and Puerto Rico
And separately he annexed Hawaii

He kept the nation on the gold standard
Thus rejecting the monetary policy of free silver
Shortly after being elected to a second term
He became the third president shot by an assassinator

THEODORE ROOSEVELT

26TH PRESIDENT
Party: Republican
1901–1909
b. 1858, d. 1919

Theodore Roosevelt welcomed the twentieth century
With an exuberant trademark "Bully"
Born in New York
He was the youngest person
To assume the presidency

In the Spanish-American War
Cuba's San Juan Hill
Fell to his Rough Rider Regiment
Making him a national hero
And shortly thereafter Vice President

Roosevelt became President
Upon McKinley's assassination
As President, he was a strong believer
In executive action

As a trustbuster, he dissolved
A giant railroad combination
He pursued a square deal for the average citizen
He fought hard for conservation

In foreign affairs Teddy
Brokered peace in the Russo-Japanese War
Began the Panama Canal
And sent the Great White Fleet
On a world tour

WILLIAM HOWARD TAFT

27TH PRESIDENT
Party: Republican
1909–1913
b. 1857, d. 1930

William Howard Taft
Was another Ohioan
He was a distinguished jurist
Effective administrator and poor politician

He preferred law to politics
And was a federal judge in his early prime
Following the Spanish-American War
He was Governor of the Philippines for a time

Taft was Secretary of War under Roosevelt
And his chosen successor
But as Taft's presidency went on
His adherence to Roosevelt's progressivism
Fell short of being strong

In the election of 1912
Roosevelt bolted the Republican Party
He ran as a Bull Moose Progressive
Which split the Republican vote
Giving Democrat Woodrow Wilson the presidency

Taft later achieved
A long-held ambition
Chief Justice of the Supreme Court
The ultimate legal recognition

WOODROW WILSON

28TH PRESIDENT
Party: Democratic
1913–1921
b. 1856, d. 1924

Woodrow Wilson was born in Virginia
Raised in Georgia and South Carolina
He was the first president from the South
Since the 1860s Brouha

He was an academic
The President of Princeton University
And a politician
The Governor of New Jersey

As a result of Roosevelt's third party
Democrat Wilson won the 1912 election
His political leanings were progressive
And his administration's style was aggressive

His administration produced lower tariffs
A federal income tax, the Federal Reserve Act
And the Federal Trade Commission
On the downside was an increase
In internal Government racial segregation

In Wilson's second term
With the rally cry of
"Make the world safe for democracy"
He led the nation into World War I
And to victory
But failed to get Congress's approval
For League of Nations membership
And the war-ending Versailles Treaty

WARREN G. HARDING

29TH PRESIDENT
Party: Republican
1921–1923
b. 1865, d. 1923

Warren G. Harding was, to date,
The last of eight Ohio residents
Who were elected
United States presidents

Before becoming a politician
Harding was a newspaper publisher
He held state offices
And eventually became a United States Senator

His 1920 presidential effort
Saw the first significant adaptions
Of many modern campaign techniques
Including newsreels, sound recordings, motion pictures
And telemarketing applications

Harding won the 1920 election
With 60 percent of the popular vote
And a return to normalcy optimism
His policies have been described
As undeviating Republicanism

He died of a heart attack in 1923
Teapot Dome and other scandals
Tarnished his administration
Leaving him with a less than stellar
Presidential reputation

CALVIN COOLIDGE

30TH PRESIDENT
Party: Republican
1923–1929
b. 1872, d. 1933

Calvin Coolidge was born in Vermont
In Massachusetts, he entered law and politics
He was distinguished more for his character
Than for his achievements

He was born on July 4
The only such White House resident
On Warren Harding's death
VP Coolidge became the President

The Roaring Twenties were a time
Of growth and prosperity
Major challenges were few
So governing was relatively easy
Which suited Silent Cal's personality

After the scandals of his predecessor
He restored confidence in the presidency
Tax cuts, limited aid to farmers, isolationism
Were components of his legacy

Silent Cal was silent
In five languages
Was one contemporary saying
About his limited verbal responses

HERBERT HOOVER

31ST PRESIDENT
Party: Republican
1929–1933
b. 1874, d. 1964

Herbert Hoover was born in Iowa
And raised in Oregon
He was a businessman, mining engineer
Administrator, humanitarian

He provided food during and after
World War I
To war-torn Europe
And became known as
The Great Humanitarian

Under Harding and Coolidge
As Secretary of Commerce
He made the department
A valuable information clearinghouse

But as President, he was
In the wrong place at the wrong time
Shortly after he took office
In 1929
The stock market crashed
And the Great Depression came online

His efforts at recovery
Were hampered by his hesitancy
To have the federal government
Participate too extensively

FRANKLIN D. ROOSEVELT

32ND PRESIDENT
Party: Democratic
1933–1945
b. 1882, d. 1945

With the nation at a low point
In 1933
Franklin Delano Roosevelt
Assumed the presidency

Born and raised in New York
FDR was a politician
He was Secretary of the Navy
Under Woodrow Wilson
And in 1928 was elected
To the New York Governor's position

On becoming President
He told the country
It had nothing to fear but fear itself
And immediately turned
To repairing the economy

Over the first eight years of his presidency
His New Deal experimented and implemented
Slowly lifting economic activity from
The depths to which it had descended

Then came World War II
Pearl Harbor and wartime mobilizations
Under FDR the United States assumed leadership
Against the Axis nations

FDR had a major physical disability but cast a giant shadow
He was the only president elected more than twice
He's often considered with Washington and Lincoln
To be the presidents of greatest distinction

HARRY S. TRUMAN

33RD PRESIDENT
Party: Democratic
1945–1953
b. 1884, d. 1972

Farmer, businessman, politician
Harry Truman was from Missouri
In World War I, he was
A Captain in the Field Artillery

Truman was elected Senator in 1934
And Vice President in 1944
Thus on Roosevelt's death in April of '45
Truman got the key to the White House door

He made the decision to drop
Atomic bombs on Japan
Thereby ending World War II
But a stable world was not at hand

He implemented the Marshall Plan
To rebuild Western Europe's economy
The Truman Doctrine and NATO
Were a response to Communist activity

He went to war in Korea
To counter a Communist invasion
But he kept the war limited
Thus forestalling possible nuclear conflagration

Through executive orders, he began
The pursuit of racial equality
In federal agencies
And the nation's military

DWIGHT DAVID EISENHOWER

34TH PRESIDENT
Party: Republican
1953–1961
b. 1890, d. 1969

Dwight David "Ike" Eisenhower
Born in Texas, raised in Kansas
Was a West Point graduate and a career soldier
He commanded the Normandy Invasion
Oversaw victory in Europe
And played golf with precision

After two decades, America was ready
In 1952
For a break with the Democratic Party
And a return to the Republican crew

Compared to what was before
And what was to come
The 1950s were
A moment in the sun

A major historic event
In 1954
Was Brown v. Board of Education
In which the Supreme Court held
The Constitution did not allow segregation

At least in theory anyway
It is taking some time
To institute the cultural change
And turn many a mind

JOHN F. KENNEDY

35TH PRESIDENT
Party: Democratic
1961–1963
b. 1917, d. 1963

John Fitzgerald Kennedy was a member
Of a noted Massachusetts family
In World War II, he commanded
PT boats in the Navy
PT 109 was rammed
By a Japanese destroyer
He led the survivors to safety

Elected to the House after the war
He later became a Senator
He wrote a book, *Profiles in Courage*
And in 1960 was the Democratic Presidential contender

Richard Nixon was his opponent
They engaged in the first presidential debates on TV
JFK's inauguration address challenged the nation:
"Ask not what your country can do for you
Ask what you can do for your country"

His term was short but eventful
The Peace Corps was founded
Soviet confrontations over Berlin and Cuba occurred
The exploration of space accelerated

The Camelot Era ended
In November of '63
JFK was assassinated
And the loss was felt deeply

LYNDON B. JOHNSON

36TH PRESIDENT
Party: Democratic
1963–1969
b. 1908, d. 1973

Lyndon Baines Johnson was a Texan
He was elected to the House in 1937
In 1948 became a US Senator
And in 1953 became the Senate Democratic Leader

In the beginning of World War II
He was briefly on active duty in the Navy
He received a Silver Star
When his plane was shot at from afar

When John Kennedy was assassinated
In November 1963
LBJ was the VP
And thus assumed the presidency

As President, he had
Both great success and great failure
The great success included
The many components
Of the Great Society
Among them voting and civil rights, Medicare
Urban renewal, and the war on poverty

The great failure was
The Vietnam morass
Into which the nation slid
Like a dog on slick glass

RICHARD NIXON

37TH PRESIDENT
Party: Republican
1969–1974
b. 1913, d. 1994

1968 was a year like few others
The Tet Offensive showed the futility of Vietnam
Martin Luther King and Robert Kennedy
Were victims of assassination
Riots erupted across the land
The Democratic convention was a chaotic absurdity
And Richard Milhous Nixon captured the presidency

Nixon was a Californian
In World War II, a Navy Lieutenant in the Pacific
He left active duty as a Lieutenant Commander
After the war, he was elected to the House
And in 1950 became a US Senator

During Eisenhower's two terms
He held the vice presidency
Performing many functions
And demonstrating the office's possibility

As President, he brought
America's Vietnam involvement
To a gradual messy termination
And improved relations with
The Soviet Union and the China nation

In 1972
Nixon was reelected in a landslide
But his involvement in nefarious political activity
Known as the Watergate scandal
Led to the first and thus far only
Resignation from the presidency

GERALD FORD

38TH PRESIDENT
Party: Republican
1974–1977
b. 1913, d. 2006

Gerald Ford was born in Nebraska
Grew up in Michigan
Was a star football player
At the University of Michigan
And was in the Navy in World War II
On an aircraft carrier in the Pacific Ocean

He left the Navy as a Lieutenant Commander
From '49 to '73 was in the US House
The last years as the Minority Leader

Nixon's Vice President was Spiro Agnew
Who resigned over financial shenanigans
Nixon selected under the Twenty-fifth Amendment
Ford as Agnew's replacement
Which was confirmed by the House and the Senate

On Nixon's resignation over the Watergate shenanigans
Ford became the first Eagle Scout to achieve the presidency
He made a political mistake by pardoning Nixon
But long term that was probably best for the nation

During Ford's two-plus years in office
The economy was buffeted by inflation and recession
Détente with the Soviets continued
And Middle East policy was aimed at war prevention

JIMMY CARTER

39TH PRESIDENT
Party: Democratic
1977–1981
b. 1924, d. living

James Earl Carter Jr.
Was the first president hospital born
That was in Georgia
Where he was raised from then on

He graduated in '46 from the Naval Academy
Served seven years on active duty
Then returned to Georgia
To fulfill a long-time dream
Of being a peanut farmer

He entered politics, was in the state legislature
And in the early '70s
Was the Governor
The national stage beckoned
And despite confessing to
Looking at many women with lust
He became President
But the times were just messy stuff

International tensions, mounting inflation
Unemployment, energy problems, stagflation
Made forward progress
A difficult proposition

Détente ended with
The Soviet invasion of Afghanistan
And Jimmy's presidency ended with
The hostage crisis in Iran

RONALD REAGAN

40TH PRESIDENT
Party: Republican
1981–1989
b. 1911, d. 2004

Ronald Reagan was the Man
At least if you were a Republican
He could do little wrong
And if he did his supporters let him move on

The Gipper was born and raised in Illinois
Became an actor in Hollywood
In World War II served stateside
In the Army Air Forces
Making training films and public appearances

He became involved in politics
And was Governor of California
Was elected President in 1980
(The first divorcée president)
And was on his way to Morning in America

Assessing Reagan's presidency
Is not a simple calculation
He cut taxes but also increased them
Said government was the problem
But had a strong administration

He contributed to Cold War victory
Rehabilitated conservatism
Balanced ideology and political realism
And renewed faith in American exceptionalism

He exuded confidence and love of country
Displayed humor and empathy
Was able to compromise divergent viewpoints
Without making opponents the mortal enemy

GEORGE H.W. BUSH

41ST PRESIDENT
Party: Republican
1989–1993
b. 1924, d. 2018

Massachusetts born
George Herbert Walker Bush
Was mostly Connecticut raised
As a Navy aviator in World War II
He flew fifty-eight missions in the Pacific
Was shot down and rescued
And received much praise

After the war he attended Yale
Finished his education
Embarked on an oil industry career
In a West Texas location

Bush became interested in politics
(His father was a Connecticut senator)
Served two terms in the House
Held several high-level positions
Including UN Ambassador and CIA Director
And was the Vice President under the Gipper

His four years in office as President
Saw many foreign affairs successes
The Cold War ended, the Soviet Union disbanded
A Panamanian dictator was ousted
And in Operation Desert Storm
From Kuwait Saddam Hussein was ejected

But domestically there was discontent
The economy was sputtering
And the Clinton campaign successfully painted Bush
As elderly and fading
(He showed uncertainty about grocery store bar coding)

BILL CLINTON

42ND PRESIDENT
Party: Democratic
1993–2001
b. 1946, d. living

Notwithstanding H. W. Bush's
Foreign affairs successes
The nation had had enough
Of moralizing Republicanism
It wanted less rigid stuff

William Jefferson Clinton
Was from Arkansas
Georgetown graduate, Rhodes Scholar
Yale Law star
And he skipped
The Vietnam War

From Governor of Arkansas
He became President
His two terms produced economic cheers
Low unemployment and inflation
And a real oddity
Three surplus budget years

The foreign affairs scene
Had no real complications
Somalia, Cuban refugees
The Balkans, Israel, and the Palestinians
Minor stuff compared to
What challenged other administrations

The most exciting events
Flowed from Slick Willie's personal situation
Certain *indiscretions* led to
Impeachment but not conviction

GEORGE W. BUSH

43RD PRESIDENT
Party: Republican
2001–2009
b. 1946, d. living

George W. Bush was the son of
George H. W. Bush
They were the second father-son team
To achieve the White House dream

George W. was Connecticut-born
And Texas-raised
Had degrees from Yale and Harvard
Was a National Guard pilot
But avoided the 'Nam's murky haze

He started in the oil industry
Invested in the Texas Rangers baseball team
Was Governor of Texas
Then the Republican's 2000 Presidential contender
The election involved hanging Florida chads
And the Supreme Court made Bush the winner

The White House dream
Turned a bit sour
It started with 9/11
For America a very dark hour

Bush responded with an Afghanistan attack
Then an unnecessary expansion to Iraq
Meanwhile taxes were cut
Federal budget deficits soared
And beginning in 2007
The Great Recession roared

BARACK OBAMA

44TH PRESIDENT
Party: Democratic
2009–2017
b. 1961, d. living

In 1619, the first African slaves
Were brought to the future nation
In 1863, Abraham Lincoln issued
The Emancipation Proclamation

Following the Civil War the 13th, 14th, and 15th Amendments
Banned slavery and set equal rights and voter protection
In 1954, the Supreme Court ruled unconstitutional
Public school segregation

In the 1960s, Civil Rights, Voting Rights, and Fair Housing
Were titles of legislation
And in 2008, Barack Hussein Obama
Became the first African American to win
A US presidential election

Obama was born in Hawaii
Raised there and in Indonesia
Was a community organizer in Chicago
And Harvard Law Review Editor

His presidency produced
More accessible and affordable health care
Financial industry oversight repair
An Iranian antinuclear treaty
And a start toward a climate change remedy

But he ran into hostility
From Republican tea party irascibility
Birthers said he was born in Kenya
Mitch McConnell sought a one-term president
Notwithstanding he was reelected
And served a second term effectively
Despite much knee-jerk puerility

DONALD J. TRUMP

45TH PRESIDENT
Party: Republican
2017–2021
b. 1946, d. living

Donald J. Trump was
A Vietnam avoider (bone spurs)
A mediocre real estate developer
A bankruptcy-prone hotel and casino operator
And a successful TV entertainer

He had autocratic tendencies
With over 30,000 whoppers was
A world class prevaricator
And with the aid of social media
Appealed to the lowest common denominator

In the election of 2016
He was second in the popular vote
But the Electoral College count
Gave him the presidential rope

His tenure was marked by
A tax cut that increased the national debt
Behavior that alienated citizens and allies alike
An impeachment effort in 2020
And a pandemic that became
A major national blight

He lost his 2020 effort at reelection
But refused to concede
He stoked a mob insurrection
That occupied the Capitol and led
To a second impeachment confrontation

JOE BIDEN

46TH PRESIDENT
Party: Democratic
2021-Present
b. 1942, d. living

Joe Biden was born in Pennsylvania
Moved to Delaware as a youngster
And eventually became
A Delaware lawyer

He was elected to the Senate
At the age of twenty-nine
Was there thirty-six years
That's quite a lot of time

He served periods as Chairman of
The Senate Foreign Relations Committee
And the Senate Judiciary Committee
He learned the ways of Washington
Both the politicians and the city
And developed an aversion
To excessive malarky

Joe ran for president in 1988
And again in 2008
He settled in that year
For being Obama's running mate

Eight years the Vice President
And then in 2021
He overcame his predecessor's plotting
To steal a presidential fraud-free election
And hit the ground running
But Afghanistan caused some stumbling

FINAL WORD

So there you have it
A quirky look at the presidents
Conclusion:
Sometimes a president will turn out well
Sometimes a president won't
Similarly with us voters
Sometimes we make an admirable choice
Sometimes we don't

ABOUT THE ILLUSTRATOR

Phil McKenney provides the quirky illustrations. He is a free-lance cartoonist/illustrator specializing in book, magazine, and newspaper work, and he provided the illustrations in David Holland's book, *Who'd You Vote For, Er...Against?* He also does courtroom illustrations for television. He currently performs a live show entitled "Wild Men, the Dawn of Rock n Roll," giving the history of that music through his art, singing, and storytelling. He is a graduate of Virginia Commonwealth University with a major in Communication Arts. He lives in Montross, in Virginia's Northern Neck region.

ABOUT THE AUTHOR

David Holland provides the quirky verse/poems. He has been a law-yer, consultant, federal government employee, and military officer. He has self-published a three-volume memoir on Vietnam (*Vietnam, a Memoir*) and books on the federal bureaucracy (*One Space or Two*), the origins of the Great Recession (*Creating Money*), and pres-idential elections (*Who'd You Vote For, Er…Against?*). He regularly posts verse to crankyoldguys.blogspot.com. His alma maters include the University of Virginia, the College of William & Mary, George Washington University, and George Mason University. He resides in Alexandria, Virginia.

CPSIA information can be obtained
at www.ICGtesting.com
Printed in the USA
JSHW031203240622
27398JS00003BA/21